My First Pony Show

J798·24

KINGFISHER

Kingfisher Publications Plc,
New Penderel House,
283–288 High Holborn,
London WC1V 7HZ
www.kingfisherpub.com

First published by Kingfisher
Publications Plc 2006
10 9 8 7 6 5 4 3 2 1
1TR/0806/SNPLFG/CLSN(CLSN)/140MA/C

ISBN-13: 978 0 7534 1348 7
ISBN-10: 0 7534 1348 5

A CIP catalogue record for this book
is available from the British Library.

Printed in China

Consultant: Elwyn Hartley Edwards
Editor: Russell Mclean
Designer: Poppy Jenkins
Photographer: Matthew Roberts
Picture research manager: Cee Weston-Baker
Senior production controller: Lindsey Scott
DTP co-ordinator: Catherine Hibbert

Roma

Dublin
Ride. Life. Style.

The Cuddly Ponies Club

Clothing and equipment supplied by
Cuddly Ponies, Dublin Clothing and
Roma (www.dublinclothing.com).

Ponies supplied and
produced by Justine
Armstrong-Small BHSAI,
pictured with Zin Zan
(Champion Working
Hunter, Horse of the Year
Show 2004; Champion
Lightweight Working
Hunter, Royal Windsor
Horse Show 2005).

My First Pony Show

Judith Draper

KINGFISHER

Contents

Showing a pony

Going to a show is one of the most exciting things you can do with your pony. You do not need a very beautiful or expensive pony to have fun and win rosettes. The most important thing is to do lots of practice first.

Hacking out

Even when you are hacking out in the country, remember to ride correctly and have your pony under control. It is good practice for when you take him to a show.

Snaffle bit

In lead-rein and first ridden pony classes, you must be able to control your pony in a simple snaffle bit.

Which competition?

There are competitions to suit all ponies and riders. Very young riders can enter lead-rein classes. There are competitions for smart riding ponies, fun gymkhana games, and show jumping too.

Gymkhana games are great fun if you have a quick, obedient pony.

If you are a confident rider you will enjoy taking part in show jumping competitions.

Good handling

Before you go to a show, practise handling your pony at home. If you are entering a showing class, you will need to show your pony to the judge at halt, walk and trot, without a saddle.

hard hat

bridle

gloves

reins

All together

Your pony must learn to be calm and well behaved in the company of other ponies. If he is not, he might become overexcited when he walks into a crowded show ring.

Safety first!

Have an older person with you when you are learning to handle your pony. You may need help at first if he becomes frisky.

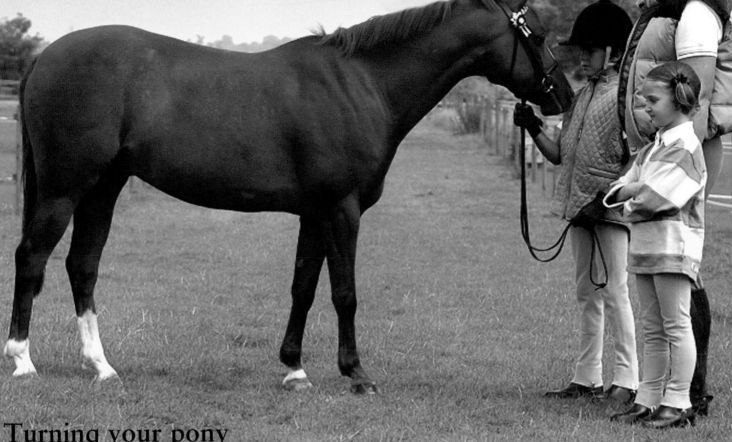

Safety first!

When you lead a pony, always pay attention so that he does not tread on your toes.

Standing square

It is important that a pony is able to stand still in the show ring. If he fidgets, ask an adult to help you train him.

Turning your pony

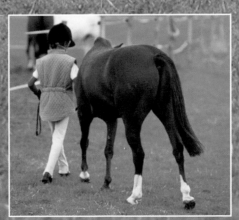

1 Hold the reins in your right hand, close to the bit rings. Use your left hand to hold the other end. Start to turn at walking pace.

2 Stay close to the pony's neck as you guide him gently round to the right. Look where you are going, not at your pony.

3 As you complete the turn, straighten up your pony so he is ready to move off again. When leading, you should be by the pony's shoulder.

Show rein

At a show, the lead rein is fastened to the underneath of a pony's noseband.

Lead-rein practice

A perfect way for a young rider to begin showing is to enter a lead-rein competition. An adult will lead your pony, but you still need to show that you have learned the basics of riding. You should know how to ask the pony to trot on and how to hold and use the reins.

look to the front

sit up tall

Perfect position

Do plenty of lead-rein practice to make sure that your position in the saddle is as good as possible.

keep your heels down

If you start to lose your balance, hold on to the saddle.

lead rein

Safety first!

Use safety stirrup irons, which release your feet quickly if you fall.

To show that the rider can control the pony, an adult leads on a loose rein. If the rider begins to lose control, the leader can help out.

Gymkhana games

To do well in gymkhana games, you need to practise at home. Make a line of cones or poles in your schooling area and weave in and out of the line, first at trot, then at canter. Try to pick up and carry items such as flags on sticks, then drop them into a bucket while you are still mounted.

Your pony needs to be able to make a fast start, so practise going from halt to canter as quickly as you can.

Safety first!
Have an adult with you when you practise, in case you need help.

Quick turn
You must be able to make quick turns without pulling your pony about. Practise turning round a cone, at trot first, then at canter.

Practise your show

At the beginning of a show class, all the ponies circle the arena together at the different paces. Then they line up in the middle and each rider gives a short individual show. You must practise this at home if you are to impress the judge.

Keep it simple

Work out a short show that includes a walk, trot and canter, and a halt. In some classes the judge will ask you to change the rein. Riding a figure-of-eight is the best way to do this.

You must teach your pony to move in a straight line. Trotting him up beside a fence will help.

To salute the judge, bow your head and straighten one arm.

Fitness work

Competing at a show can be hard work, so build up your pony's fitness at home. Start gently, with walking and slow trotting. Too much fast work too soon could injure your pony's legs.

Riding up hills is one of the best ways to improve your pony's fitness.

If your pony is fit, he will be able to keep going in a relaxed canter without you having to kick him on.

Gallop

In some competitions you will need to gallop. Make sure that your pony is fit enough and that you can control him at speed.

A flash noseband gives the rider extra control. The lower strap helps to stop the pony from opening his mouth and avoiding the bit.

A running martingale stops your pony from carrying his head too high. It is fitted to the girth at one end and the reins at the other.

Keep your head up and look forwards to the next fence.

Be careful not to use the reins to keep your balance.

Keep your lower legs under you – do not let them swing back.

The poles rest on supports called 'cups'. These slot into special stands.

Riding over trotting poles is the first step for beginners who are learning to jump.

Jumping

There are jumping competitions for riders of all ages and ponies of all sizes. Before you enter one you should practise your jumping position at home. You must be able to ride your pony round a short course of different jumps.

Safety first!
You should wear a body protector when you are jumping, to protect your back if you have a fall.

Cross country
If you are a really good rider you may enjoy jumping cross-country fences. Unlike show jumps, these do not fall down if the pony hits them.

Cross-pole fence
A simple cross-pole fence is ideal for jumping practice. The crossed poles encourage the pony to jump over the middle of the fence. You can raise the height of the poles gradually.

Jump over different coloured fences so that your pony will not be nervous, or 'spooky', when you take him to a show.

Upright fence
When you are happy jumping cross-poles you can start to jump the sort of small fences that you will find at a show. This is an upright fence. The pony is folding his front legs well out of the way.

Food and water

If you ride your pony often, you may need to give him 'hard' feed, such as a coarse mix or pony nuts. These will provide him with more energy than just grass and hay. Ask an experienced person, such as your riding instructor, to work out a diet for your pony.

Safety first!
Never water or feed your pony just before or straight after a competition.

manger

Food in the field
When your pony is out at grass, you can feed him from a special 'manger' that fastens onto a fence rail. Do not give him too much, because he may become overexcited.

Feeding at a show

Ponies like to eat at the same time each day. But if you are going to a show you may have to change your pony's routine. Make sure he has his usual morning feed. Get up extra early if necessary so that there is time for his food to go down before you set off.

If you give your pony the right food in the weeks before a show, he will have a shiny coat and be full of energy for the competition.

Feed bowl

The natural way for your pony to eat is on the ground. In the stable, put his feed in a plastic bowl.

If you are travelling a long way to a show, take a haynet for the pony to nibble at on the way home or during any long gaps between competitions.

Take a large container of fresh water to the show so that your pony can have a drink when he needs one.

Bathing and trimming

Your pony must look really clean and smart for a show. A very dirty pony may need to be washed all over. You should bathe and trim him the day before the show. Then put a rug on your pony to keep him clean overnight.

1 Wash your pony's head with a sponge. Be gentle, avoiding his eyes and ears. Use a mild shampoo that does not irritate his skin.

2 Make sure that you rinse off all the shampoo. A hosepipe is ideal for this job.

3 Use a sweat scraper to remove any water from his neck and body.

4 Carefully remove any tangles from his mane and tail with a mane comb.

headcollar

Drying off

After a bath, walk your pony until he is dry.
If you let him stand still, he might catch a chill.
A light cooler rug helps him to dry more quickly.

Safety first!

An older, more experienced person should always trim your pony. They should use round-ended scissors to avoid injuring him if he moves suddenly. If your pony becomes fed-up or fidgety, tie him up with a quick-release knot.

Trimming

Ask an adult to trim off some of the pony's mane behind the ears, where the bridle fits.

Round-ended scissors must be used to carefully trim your pony's whiskers.

If your pony has hairy heels, they will look neater if the long hairs are snipped off.

Plaiting

A plaited mane and tail make a pony look extra smart. The mane is pulled first so that it is not too long or thick. The tail must be left unpulled.

rolled-up
mane plait

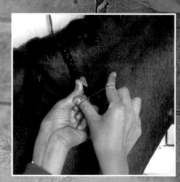

Top tip

Needle and thread

For smart shows, forelock and mane plaits are fastened with a needle and thread to give a neater finish. Ask an adult to help you.

Plaiting the mane

  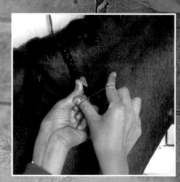

1 Dampen the mane and divide the hair into an uneven number of equal-sized bunches – nine or eleven, for example.

2 Divide each bunch of mane hair into three equal strands. Then plait the strands together tightly and neatly.

3 Wind a rubber band round the end of the plait. Fold the plait into a ball and fasten it securely with the rubber band.

finished
tail plait

Plaiting the tail

1 Dampen the hair.
Then take small
bunches from either
side and plait them
together with a small
number of hairs from
the middle of your
pony's dock.

2 Carry on plaiting
down the dock in
this way. Take care
to use equal-sized
bunches of hair and
keep the plait in the
middle of the dock.

3 Plait the hair to
three-quarters of
the way down the
dock. Keep plaiting,
but do not take in
any more new hair.

4 Ask an adult to
help you fasten
the end of the plait
with a needle and
thread. Then fold the
finished plait under
itself and sew it
firmly in place.

21

Ready to travel

There is a lot to remember when you are getting ready for a show. Make a list of everything you need to do and another of all the items you need to take. Clean the trailer or horsebox, the pony's tack and travelling equipment, and your clothes too. Don't forget to pack your pony's vaccination certificate and passport.

Safety first!
Always tie up your pony when you are getting him ready to travel. Try to keep him calm too.

Groom your pony the day before the show, and bathe him if he is dirty. Leave plenty of time to groom him again on the morning of the show.

Prepare all your tack in advance. It should look as clean and shiny as possible. Check that all the stitching and buckles are secure.

Bandage your pony's tail before you set off, to stop him rubbing it on the journey. Ask an adult to check that the bandage is not too tight.

Check your list as you pack each item. Remember to take spare tack in case anything breaks.

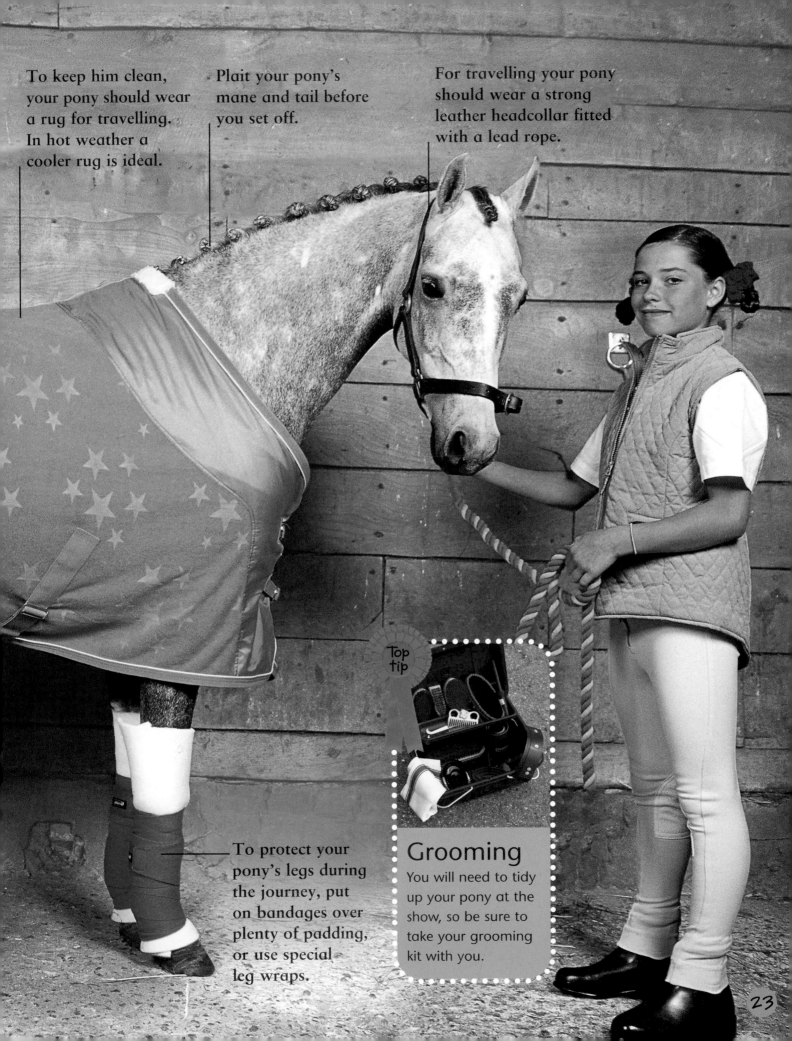

To keep him clean, your pony should wear a rug for travelling. In hot weather a cooler rug is ideal.

Plait your pony's mane and tail before you set off.

For travelling your pony should wear a strong leather headcollar fitted with a lead rope.

Top tip

To protect your pony's legs during the journey, put on bandages over plenty of padding, or use special leg wraps.

Grooming

You will need to tidy up your pony at the show, so be sure to take your grooming kit with you.

23

Loading practice

If your pony has not travelled for a while, practise loading and unloading him a few times before a show. Put the lights on in the trailer or box.

Going to the show

Going into a trailer or horsebox is all part of a pony's routine when he goes to a show. Most ponies quickly get used to loading and unloading and do not seem to mind the travelling. Even the calmest pony must wear leg protectors. If your trailer or box has a low roof, fit a poll guard to your pony's headcollar to protect the top of his head.

Helping hand

Ask an adult to load your pony for you. They should walk beside his shoulder and lead him up the ramp in a straight line.

side door

cooler rug

tail bandage

travel bandage

A confident pony will walk calmly up the ramp without rushing. The ramp must rest on level ground.

Take a shovel and broom with you for removing droppings at the show. Always clean the horsebox when you get home.

A trailer is smaller than a horsebox and is towed by another vehicle. The driver must drive smoothly so that the pony does not lose his balance.

A horsebox is a motorized vehicle that can carry several horses or ponies. Some have living space for people at the front.

Safety first!

Stand well out of the way when your pony is being loaded. If something startles him, he might swerve to the side of the ramp.

Finishing touches

Always arrive at a show early so there is plenty of time for your pony to relax and for you to tidy him up after the journey. Remove his travelling gear, check him over and groom him. Make sure his plaits are neat and tidy. You will need an assistant to help you with the finishing touches just before you begin your competition.

Clean round your pony's eyes and nose with a damp sponge. If he has dark skin, wipe a little baby oil round his muzzle to make it look shiny.

Remove any stains from white legs with a damp sponge. Brush a little chalk into the hair to make white markings appear even whiter.

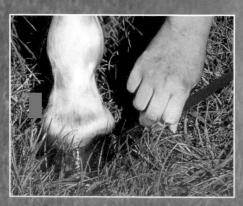

Clean any dirt from the hooves and brush on a little hoof oil. For the best effect, do this just before your pony goes into the show ring.

Safety first!

Always have an adult helper with you to hold your pony while you tack him up and apply the finishing touches.

Quarter marks

A show pony looks especially elegant with decorative 'quarter marks' on his hindquarters. You can make them with a brush or a special comb.

27

Warming up

Before you go in for a competition, make sure that your pony is well warmed up. This is especially important if he has been standing in a horsebox or trailer during a long journey. Always warm up at the different paces, beginning with walk.

Do a little practice before a show jumping competition, but do not tire out your pony. There is no need to make the fences very high.

When you are warming up in the collecting ring, always pass riders who are coming the other way left side to left side.

Once you have warmed your pony up at walk and trot, you can do some slow cantering.

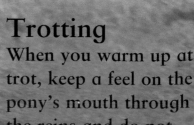

Trotting

When you warm up at trot, keep a feel on the pony's mouth through the reins and do not let him rush along.

hard hat

Make sure that your position in the saddle is correct.

gloves

jodhpur boots

Relaxed pony

Your pony will perform best when he is relaxed but still keen. It takes practice to know how much warming up each pony needs.

Top tip

Looking good

Just before you go into the show ring, ask your helper to check that you and your pony look as smart as possible.

29

Fun and games

Mounted games are great fun for both riders and ponies. There are games for riders of all levels, from lead-rein upwards. In many races, things must be moved from one place to another, so riders need good coordination and obedient ponies.

Water race

In this competition, each rider uses a beaker to carry water from a container at the far end of the course to another container at the start. When the final whistle is blown, the winner is the rider who moved the most water.

You do not need a smart, showy pony to do well at mounted games. Agility and speed are more important than good looks!

Jumping races

If you like jumping and your pony is very obedient, you will enjoy the bucket race. After each round, one bucket is removed. If your pony knocks over a bucket or refuses to jump, you are eliminated.

Top tip

Go straight

The fewer the buckets, the harder they are to jump. Aim straight for the middle to stop your pony running out to the side.

These coloured buckets look small, but your pony must be well trained to jump this type of obstacle.

Bending race

In this competition, the riders canter up a line of poles or cones, weaving round each one in turn. At the end of the line they turn round quickly and ride back down the line, still weaving in and out. Bending races can be for single riders or for teams.

Safety first!

Be careful not to turn your pony too sharply when you are racing. He might slip and fall.

Sturdy traffic cones are often used instead of bending poles. ⎯⎯⎯

Stepping stone race

The rider gallops to a line of buckets, jumps off and runs along the top. At the end of the line they remount, go round a marker and repeat the bucket dash on the way back. The rider must be back in the saddle, with a leg on either side of the pony, before reaching the finish.

You need good balance and a well-behaved pony to do well in a stepping stone race.

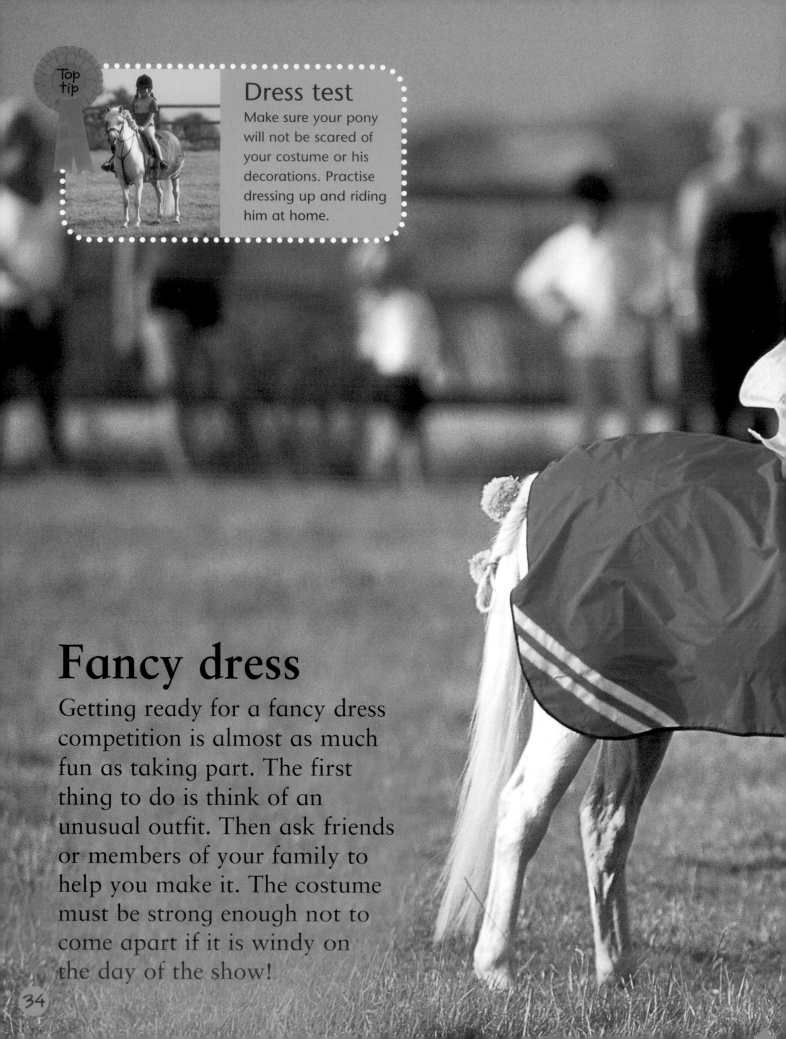

Dress test

Make sure your pony will not be scared of your costume or his decorations. Practise dressing up and riding him at home.

Fancy dress

Getting ready for a fancy dress competition is almost as much fun as taking part. The first thing to do is think of an unusual outfit. Then ask friends or members of your family to help you make it. The costume must be strong enough not to come apart if it is windy on the day of the show!

Like this rider, you can decorate your hat to make it look more pretty.

Coloured woollen pompoms are very eye-catching. They are easy to make and you can fasten them to your pony's mane and tail.

Jodhpurs
You need to be safe and comfortable in the saddle, so it is best to wear jodhpurs under your costume.

Safety first!
Always wear a well-fitting riding hat and jodhpur boots.

Walking the course

Walking the course is a very important part of show jumping. Walk with a more experienced rider who can point out problems and suggest how to solve them. You should walk the exact line that you plan to ride, without cutting corners.

Numbers

When you are in the collecting ring before the show, listen out for your number, then trot or canter into the arena.

Each fence has a number. Walk the course in the right order to help you memorize it. You will be eliminated if you jump the wrong course.

Spooky fences

Watch out for any strange-looking fences. You must not show them to the pony before you start your round, but you are allowed to ride past them. When you ask your pony to jump them, he will not be taken by surprise.

Two fences close together are called a double. Work out the number of pony strides between them by measuring your own stride. Then count the steps you take between the two fences. A pony's canter stride is usually three metres. He lands and takes off half a stride from each fence. So a one-stride distance between two fences is six metres. A two-stride distance is nine metres.

If you want to doublecheck the distance between two fences, go back and count your steps again.

The first fence on a show jumping course for beginner riders is always an easy one, such as this little cross-pole fence.

This type of fence is called a wall. It is made of special hollow bricks that fall off easily if your pony touches them.

If your pony has a refusal, circle round and jump the fence again. If he knocked it down, you must wait while it is rebuilt.

Top tip

Under way

After the bell rings, you have 45 seconds before you must cross the start line.

Show jumping

There are show jumping competitions to suit all sizes of pony and all ages of rider. For beginners, clear-round classes are ideal. Everyone who jumps the whole course successfully receives a rosette and there is no jump-off. Your pony must be well schooled to enter the competition.

When you jump one fence, you should already be looking ahead to the next. If your pony knocks down a pole, do not let it put you off – you cannot do anything about it.

Always ride at the centre of each fence.

The jump-off

In some competitions, the riders who have a clear round go into a jump-off against the clock. This is over a shorter course, which you must memorize by studying the plan in the collecting ring. Sometimes, jumping at an angle can save time.

Lead-rein classes

For inexperienced riders aged from three to seven, lead-rein competitions are the perfect introduction to showing. At very big shows, only the pony is judged. At smaller shows, both the pony and the skill of the rider are judged. The pony is led by an adult.

Good manners are important at a show. Always salute the judge by smiling and nodding your head.

Your pony must be used to standing still while he is examined by the judge. Your leader helps by standing in front of the pony.

Each rider and pony must give a simple individual show at walk and trot.

After your individual show, remember to pat your pony to say thank you.

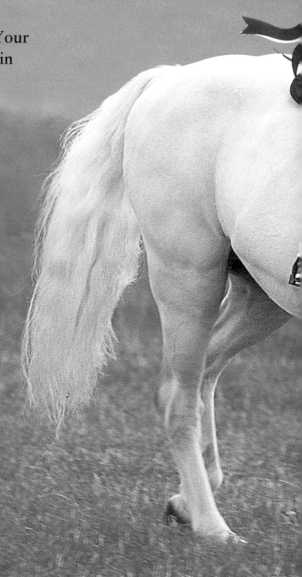

Prize giving

If you are lucky enough to win first prize or be placed, you will receive a rosette and a prize. A small rosette can be fastened to your pony's bridle. Wherever you finish, remember to keep smiling!

— sash

— rosette

Safety first!
If your pony is nervous, you can pin a rosette to your show jacket.

First ridden pony

First ridden pony classes are for riders who are experienced enough to be off the lead-rein and ponies that are less than 12 hands high.

After the ride round, the judge's assistant, who is known as the steward, calls the riders in to form a line.

Round the ring

At the beginning of the class, all the ponies are ridden round the show ring, first at walk and then at trot.

Your pony is judged on his 'conformation' (his overall shape and how he is put together), how he moves and how well he can be ridden by a young person.

Make sure the judge can see you by not riding next to another pony.

Safety first!
If your pony becomes overexcited, leave the show ring quietly.

Your show

Then the steward asks each rider to do a short show. Work this out at home and do plenty of practice. It should include walk, trot and canter, a simple change of rein (figure-of-eight), and a halt.

Make sure that your pony stands still while the judge is looking at him. Sit up tall and stay alert.

The judge will be looking for a happy pony whose ears are pricked forwards.

If the judge asks to see your pony being trotted in hand, keep him straight and do not drag him along.

After the ridden shows, the judge may ask to see each pony without his saddle. An assistant can help you to unsaddle and saddle up again.

After the prize-giving, the riders who won a rosette trot round the show ring in single file. This is called a lap of honour.

Dressage

This sport is designed to prove that a pony is well trained and that the rider has good control. Each rider has to perform the same sequence of movements at different paces. These are called a dressage test. The pony is marked out of ten for each movement.

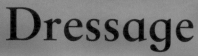

Most ponies are naturally stiffer on one side than the other. It shows that your pony is well trained if he circles well in both directions.

Good impression

The judges give a special mark for the overall impression that the rider makes.

sit up and look forwards

gloves

keep your heels down

Remember that you should only use a snaffle bit in a dressage test.

Each test begins and ends with the competitor riding down the centre line towards the judges.

All dressage tests include changes of rein which show that a pony goes equally well on both the left and right reins.

After the final halt, nod your head and salute each judge before you walk out of the arena.

Transitions

A change from one pace to another is a 'transition'. Make it as smooth as you can.

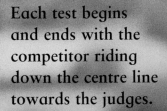

Calling your test

If you find it hard to memorize your test, check the rules to see if someone can call out each movement.

Top tip

At the end of the test, special marks are given for the way the pony goes – his paces, power and obedience.

A day off

To thank your pony for his efforts, always give him a rest on the day after a show. If he lives in a field, turn him out to graze as usual. If he is kept stabled for much of the time, lead him out in his field and let him pick at the grass.

Top tip

Pony care

Before you decide to have your own pony, remember that caring for a pony is a big responsibility. Even when he is resting after a show, he still needs looking after!

Use a strong headcollar and a long lead rope.

Glossary

Avoiding the bit
When a pony opens his mouth wide, crosses his jaws or puts his tongue over the bit, it is known as avoiding (or evading) the bit. He becomes difficult to control.

Changing the rein
Changing the direction in which you are riding.

Cups
Small supports that are attached to the side stands of a fence. The ends of the poles rest on the cups, which can be moved up or down to change the height of the fence.

Flash noseband
A noseband with an extra strap which is fitted below the rings of the bit. It helps to stop a pony opening his mouth too wide and getting out of control.

Gymkhana
An event with mounted competitions and games, such as bending races or stepping stone races.

Hacking out
Going for a ride out in the countryside.

Hands
Traditionally, horses and ponies are measured in hands. One hand equals 10 centimetres, which is roughly the width of an adult's hand.

Hoof oil
Special oil that is brushed onto a pony's hooves for very smart occasions.

Lead rein
A strong single rein that is fitted to the underside of a pony's noseband. It is used by a handler to lead the pony in classes for young, beginner riders.

Manger
A container from which a pony eats his food. In a stable the manger may be fixed to the wall. A grass-kept pony can be fed from a movable manger which clips onto a fence rail.

Poll
The top of a pony's head.

Poll guard
A piece of padded leather that fits onto the headcollar and protects the top of a pony's head when he is travelling.

Quarter marks
Patterns that are put on a pony's hindquarters by brushing or combing the hair in different directions.

Rest day
The day after a show, when a pony is not ridden.

Round-ended scissors
These are used to trim untidy hair from a pony's legs and head, and for shortening his tail.

Running martingale
A strap that helps the rider to control a pony. One end passes between the pony's front legs and is attached to the girth. The other end divides in two, and has a ring at each end to pass the reins through.

Transition
A change of pace, such as from walk to trot, trot to canter or canter back to trot. In a dressage test the judge looks for transitions that are smooth, not jerky.

Travel bandage
A wide bandage fitted over thick padding to stop a pony hurting his legs in the horsebox or trailer.

Index

Acknowledgements

The publisher would like to thank the following for their help in the production of this book:

Models: Alexis, Amy, Charley, Charlotte, Ciara, Elliot, Farren, Fraser, Hollie, Imogen, India, Justice, Leanne, Lucy, Raija, Rhianna and Simi

Ponies: Cracker, Denzel, Jasper, Pickwick, Pie, Rosie, Scamp, Big Scamp, Teddy, Teggy, Tiger

Rachel Ablett, Lisa Benton, Pat Seager and Anthony Wright

The Justine Armstrong-Small team (www.armstrong-small.co.uk): Justine and Hazel Armstrong-Small
Grooms: Becky, Katie, Lisa and Vicky

Harolds Park Farm Riding Centre

Cuddly Ponies, Dublin Clothing and Roma (www.dublinclothing.com)

All photographs by Matthew Roberts (www.matthewrobertsphotographer.com) with the exception of: page 25tr (Bob Langrish, www.boblangrish.co.uk)